LOCAL

WILLIAM WILSON
COACHING IN LAKELAND

A facsimile reprint, with new introduction, of "Coaching: past and present", by William Wilson of the Keswick Hotel. First published by J. Garnett of Windermere in 1885.

LOCAL HISTORY

D| 338.322

Carel Press
13, Bowman Street
CARLISLE
Cumbria
0-9509096-0-2
© 1983

Introduction

The reappearance of this scarce work will be welcomed by a wide audience. Students, both of transport history and Lakeland life, will find this book a unique source of material. Mr. Wilson's lively anecdotal style will also recommend him to the more casual reader.

William Wilson was born on January 19th 1836, the eldest son of George Wilson of Armboth, near Thirlmere. William's lifelong interest in horses and other country pursuits may be traced back to his early farming days. In 1875 he left the farm and bought the "Royal Oak Hotel" in Keswick. Nine years later he sold it and became lessee of the "Keswick Hotel", the most modern hotel in the county. This hotel was built by the Cockermouth, Keswick and Penrith Railway Company, and opened to the public in 1869. For many years the hotel offered the finest food, services and facilities in the North West of England. It offered plenty of scope for Wilson's boundless enterprise. While lessee he was responsible for increasing the facilities for posting in Lakeland and offered organised and regular trips for tourists by coach.

A keen traveller himself, he visited the World's Columbian Exposition in Chicago in 1893, and wrote an account of it for the Newcastle Weekly Chronicle to which he was a regular contributor. While visiting the Paris Exhibition he was taken ill and died on October 8th 1900. He was buried at Crosthwaite Church beside his daughter who had drowned in Ullswater.

I would like to thank Margaret Higginson who most kindly provided the biographical information on William Wilson. I would also like to thank Cumbria County Library who generously allowed the use of their copy of William Wilson's work for this facsimile reprint.

S.W.
5/9/83

KESWICK HOTEL, AND SKIDDAW.

COACHING, PAST AND PRESENT.

The old coaching system, as experienced by our ancestors, is no doubt a thing of the past. Of late years, however, there has been what is termed a revival of coaching in some parts of the kingdom. In the Lake District the connecting link was never entirely broken, as coaches, since their introduction, have always kept running between Windermere and Keswick, with the exception of an occasional stop for a few months during the winter season. We still have men among us who have had experience of coaching during its palmy days, and who can interest us with the adventures on the road before horse-power gave way to steam, and road was superseded by rail. No doubt many pleasant recollections are attached to the old style of travelling by four-in-hand, which people, who must now be aged, love to talk of, inasmuch as it is now nearly fifty years since the old coaching system had to give way to our present more expeditious mode of travelling. To form an idea of the difficulties which had to be contended with in the early days of coaching, we need only read a description of the road given by writers of the time, which show that only in some localities could wheel conveyances be used at all. Travelling was usually performed on horseback by those who could afford it; a man and his wife often rode together on the same horse. Merchandise was also conveyed from place to place on the backs of horses. Bearing these facts in mind, it can hardly be doubted that of all great improvements for which the present century will, in future times be noted, that in travelling must stand pre-eminent.

MALLY MESSENGER,

Who is still remembered in Keswick, walked up to London and back three times. The following is an extract from the obituary of the *Derwentwater Record* August 4th, 1856: 'At Keswick on Monday, the 4th inst, at the advanced age of 93 years, Mary

Messenger, better known to the townspeople as auld Mally Messenger. If not one of the celebrities, the deceased was at least one of the notabilities of the place. Several times during last century she performed the journey between her native place, Keswick, and London on foot, and on one occasion brought a stand table over her shoulder, an achievement which she frequently spoke of in her later years when speaking in disparagement of the effeminacy of modern manners and fashions. She maintained her sight and other faculties unimparied until within a short time of her decease. At the age of 90 years she kept a school for children, and laboured daily to teach the young idea how to shoot. On one occasion when returning from London, auld Mally was passed by a Keswick man on horseback. After a few words with her, he said 'Good day, Mally. I'll tell them in Keswick you're coming.' Whether the horseman made his calls too frequent, or his rests too long, deponent sayeth not, but the old lady used frequently to tell with great glee how she beat him home to Keswick. The distance from Keswick to London is 286 miles by the old coach road.

TO LONDON AND BACK ON HORSEBACK.

An ancestor of the Curwens of Workington Hall—Henry Curwen, gives an account of his ride from Workington to London on horseback, in September, 1726. The journey seems to have occupied about 13 days, allowing four days for visiting friends by the way. The road is described as being very bad and he considers a ride of 32 miles distance to be equal to 50 measured miles. The following is from his diary. A ride to London in 1726. Things put in my box:—5 Shirts Writings 2 Books Sword Cane 1 Pr Silver Spurs 7 Stocks 4 Handks 6 Silver Spoons 2 Silver Candlesticks 1 Pr Sheet 1 Pr Sheet Account Books 1 Pr Splator Darcos 2 Shirts (Mr. Newnham's) 6 Buck Skins September 8. Set out from Workington called at Cockermth Dined at Keswick Lay at Penrith Rid 26 miles ye new Church at Penrith the pillers of stone being all of one ps 4 yds. High 20 pillers in all Round 1 yd 5s 9d September 9 Dined at my Lord Lonsdales Lay at ye Kings head Appelby 10 miles 10 Stopt at Bruff and drank a tanket of ale alighted

at Spitle House on Stainmore   Stayed an Hower Stopt at
Greata Bridge and Drank 2 Muggs of ale Lay at the Bull in
Katricd Lane Rid 32 miles this day near 50 Mesurd Miles Bad
Road   11 Stoped at House Drank a Tankard of ale Dined at
Goulden Lyon at Helperby Lay at Mr Thompson's at the George
in York Rid 32 miles abt 50 mesurd miles   12 Monday writ
four Letters See the Minster Dined at the George had Mr
Foster to dinner went with him and drank a bottle at his house
Viseted Lady Lawson and her daughter Malley ; went with
them to Mrs Lataces went to the Asembly played at Whist
Lost 2s 6d Stayed till 12 Lay at ye George   13 Tusday See the
Castell and Jale ye Gale is the finest I ever saw Dined at ye
George went to ye play with Lady Lawson and Coasen Mary.
See the Yoeman of Kent   14th Wednesday stopt at Tedcaster
had one pint of wine took leeve of of cousen Stanley and my
Brother went on without Stoping to Doncaster Lay at the An-
gell Rid 28 miles Bad Road   15 Thursday from Doncaster to
Sir Geo Saviles 19 miles Dined 16 with Sr George Lay there
that night dined with him on Friday the 16th Lay at ye White
Lyon at Nottingham Good Road   17 Saturday Mounted at
Nottingham half an hower after 11 came to Lester to ye Crane
being 6 howers Riding 16 miles the ways being very Bad had
Mr Simpson his two sons Mr Hennel and Mr Lewis to super
with me   18 Sunday Breakfasted with Mr Simpson went to
Meeting with him Dined with him went to St Martin's Church
in ye afternoon Supt with Mr Simpson   19 Monday set out
from Lewster at 6 aclock accompined by Mr John Simpson who
carried me over the fields to Harbro 12 miles by which we mist
all ye Bad Roads Stayed with him at the Swan at Harbro an
hower & half then Past through Northampton without Stoping
se on to Newport Pannell Lay at the Swan ; Rid this day 34
miles which is about 50 mesurd miles   Got in at 5 aclock ye
roads from Harbrough to Newport are Indifrent being a hard
way   20 Tusday Set out from Newport Pannell at 9 aclock Rid
without Stoping to the Uper Red Lyon in St Albens came in at
3 Rid this day 24 miles all good way Lay at ye Uper Red Lyon
21 Wednesday alighted at the Green Man at Barnet Stayed 4
Howers None came to meet me but Mr Parks arived in ye
Evning for London

Drawn & Eng^d by W.Banks & Son. Edin^r

STOCKGHYLL FORCE, AMBLESIDE

In the Grounds of the Salutation Hotel

Arthur Young, in his six weeks' tour through the southern countries of England and Wales, complains bitterly of the execrable state of the roads. In Essex he found the ruts of incredible depth, and uses strong language at one near Tilbury. 'Of all the cursed roads,' he says, 'that ever disgraced this kingdom in the very ages of barbarism, none ever equalled that from Billoricay to the King's Head at Tilbury ; it was for near 12 miles so narrow that a mouse cannot pass any carriage. I saw a fellow creep under a waggon to assist me to lift, if possible, my chase over a hedge. To add to all the infamous circumstances that plague a traveller I must not forget the eternally meeting of the chalk waggons, themselves frequently stuck fast till a collection of them are in the same situation, and twenty or thirty horses may be tacked to each to draw out one by one.' Yet will it be believed, the proposal to form a turnpike road from Chelmsford to Tilbury was resisted by the Bruins of the country, whose horses were worried to death by bringing chalk along these vile roads. From Newham to Chepstow the road is described as being so hilly, that, to form a clear idea of it, you must suppose the country to represent the roofs of houses joined and the road to go across them. Passing further, our traveller is still more indignant, and continues : 'But my dear sir, what am I to say of the roads of this country, the turnpikes as they have the assurance to call them, and the hardest to make one pay for ? From Chepstow, to the half-way house between Newport and Bardiff, they continue to be mere rocky lanes, full of hugeous stones as big as one's horse, and abominable holes ; the first six miles from Newport were as detestable and without direction posts or mile stones, that I could not well persuade myself I was on the turnpike, but had mistook the road, and therefore asked every one I met, who answered me in my astonishment, ya-as. Whenever business carries you into this country, avoid it, at least till they have good roads, if they were good, travelling would be pleasant.' Some time afterwards Arthur Young visited the northern countries, where it appears he found things equally unsatisfactory in regard to roads. Between Richmond and Darlington, he found them 'like to dislocate his bones,' being broken in many places and almost impassable. He grows furious over the roads in Lancashire, and thus expresses himself. I know not in the whole range of language, terms sufficiently expressive to describe this infernal road. Let me most seriously caution all travellers who may accidentally propose to travel this terrible country, to avoid it as they would the devil, for a thousand to one they break their necks or their limbs or overthrows or breakings down. They will here meet with ruts four feet deep and floating with mud only from a wet summer, what must they be in winter? the only mending it receives is tumbling in some loose stones, which serve no other purpose than jolting a carriage in the most intolerable manner; there are not merely opinions but facts, for I actually passed three carts broken down in these eighteen miles of execrable memory.' When we consider the state of the roads as described by the writer I have just quoted from, it is not surprising that pack horses were generally preferred for the transport of merchandise.

THE INTRODUCTION OF COACHES.

We read of coaches being used in England as early as the year 1580, but it was only a few roads leading from the metropolis that were practicable for them. Queen Elizabeth was one of the first to start a coach. This royal vehicle was introduced by the Queen's own coachman, one Booner, a Dutchman. It is described as being little better than a cart without springs, the body resting solid upon the axles; and taking the bad roads and ill paved streets into consideration, it must have been an excessively painful means of travelling. At one of the first audiences the Queen gave to the French Ambassador in 1568, she feelingly described to him the aching pains she had suffered in consequence of being knocked about in a coach that had been driven a little too fast only a few days previously. Before the Queen turned out in her coach it was usual to send labourers and masons to mend the roads, and to render the bridges at least temporarily secure. One of these journeys, it is said, was marvellous for ease and expedition; for such was the perfect evenness of the highway that her Majesty left the coach only once while the hinds and folks of a base sort lifted it on with their poles. Although the coaches of those days were hardly so good as our waggons, their owners were proud of them, and they excited great wonder. It is related of that 'valiant knight,' Sir Henry Sydney, that on a certain day in the year 1583, he entered Shrewsbury in his waggon, with his trumpeter blowing: very joyful to behold and see. In the year 1672 there were but six coaches running in all the kingdom. A pamphlet was written and published by Mr. John Crisset, of the Charterhouse, urging their suppression, and amongst the grave reasons given for their continuance was the following :— 'These stages make gentlemen come to London on every small occasion, which otherwise they would not do but upon urgent necessity, nay, the convenience of the passage makes their wives often go up who, rather than come such long journeys on horseback would stay at home. Then when they come to town they must presently be in the mode to get fine clothes, go to plays and treats, and by these means get such a habit of idleness and love of pleasure as makes them uneasy ever after, and they must have all from London whatever it costs.' To show the magnitude of the evil the writer goes on to say that between London and the towns of York, Chester, and Exeter, not fewer than eighteen persons, making the journey in five days, travelled by them weekly, the coaches running thrice in the week, and a like number back, which came on the whole to 1,872 (passengers) in a year. The writer complains bitterly of the discomfort of travelling by coach compared with the more noble way of travelling on horseback, without advantage to men's health and business, crippled by their crowd of boxes and bundles, and forced to wade up to their knees in mire and afterwards sit in the cold till teams of horses can be sent to pull the coach out, and endure all manner of rudeness. He, indeed, presents a formidable list of objections quite as bad or worse than George Stephenson had to contend with on the introduction of railways.

AN EARLY COACH NOTICE.

The following notice was posted in York in regard to the running of Coaches which carried the mails :—

York Four Days'
Stage-Coach.

Begins on Friday *the 22th* of April, 1706.

ALL that are desirous to pass from *London* to *York*, or from *York* to *London* or any other place on that Road ; Let them Repair to the *Black Swan* in *Holbourn* in *London*, and to the *Black Swan* in *Coney-street*, in *York*.

At both which places they may be received in a Stage Coach every *Monday, Wednesday*, and *Friday*, which performs the whole Journey in Four Days, *(If God permits.)* And sets forth at Five in the Morning.

And returns from *York* to *Stamford* in two days, and from *Stamford* by *Huntington* to *London* in two days. Allowing each Passenger 14*l.* weight, and all above 3*d.* a Pound.

Performed By { *Benjamin Kingmann,*
Henry Harrison,
Walter Baynes,

Also this gives Notice that Newcastle Stage Coach sets out from York every Monday and Friday, and from Newcastle every Monday and Friday.

LIMITED COMFORTS.

Mr. Pennant writes an account of his journey in the Chester Stage to London in 1739-40. The first day, says he, we got from Chester to Whitechurch, twenty miles ; the second day to the Welsh Harp, the third to Coventry, the fourth to Northampton, the fifth to Dunstable, and as a wondrous effect, on the last to London before the commencement of night. The strain and labour of six good horses, sometimes eight, drew us through the sloughs of Mireden and many others. We were constantly out two hours before day, and as late at night, and in the depth of winter proportionately late. The coaches in those days carried but six passengers as a full load. They were all seated in the carriage. The number of accidents made it dangerous to sit on the roof. The fare was about twopence halfpenny per mile in summer, and somewhat more in winter. This mode of travelling, says Macauley, which by Englishmen of the present day would be regarded as insufferably slow, seemed to our ancestors wonderfully and indeed alarmingly rapid; for, in a work published a few months before the death of Charles II., the flying coaches are extolled to any similar vehicles ever known in the world. Their velocity is the subject of special commendation, and is triumphantly contrasted with the sluggish pace of the continental posts, but with boasts like these were mingled the sound of complaint and invective.

THE DILIGENCE.

The interest of large classes had been unfavourably affected by the establishment of the diligencies, and as usual many persons were, from mere stupidity and obstinacy, clamouring against the innovation. It was vehemently argued that the mode of conveyance would be fatal to the breed of horses, and to the noble art of horsemanship; that the Thames that had long been an important nursery of seamen would cease to be the chief thoroughfare from London up to Windsor and down to Gravesend; that saddlers and spurriers would be ruined by the hundred; that numerous inns where travellers had been in the habit of stopping at would be deserted, and could no longer pay the rent; that the new carriages were too hot in summer and too cold in winter; that the passengers were greviously annoyed by invalids and crying children; that the coach sometimes reached the inn so late that it was impossible to get supper, and sometimes started so early that it was impossible to get breakfast. On these grounds it was gravely recommended that no public carriage should be permitted to have more than four horses, to start oftener than once a week, or to go more than thirty miles a day. It was hoped that if this regulation were adopted all except the sick and the lame would return to the old modes of travelling on horseback and by water. Petitions embodying such opinions as these were presented to the King in Council from several companies of the city of London, from provincial towns, and from the justices of several counties. Sir Walter Scott speaks of the northern diligence as a huge old-fashioned tub. This vehicle was drawn by three horses, and, in 1745, was accustomed to accomplish the distance between Edinburgh and London in three weeks.

C O N I S T O N

from the wood above Bank ground

L. Aspland Delt.   W. Banks Sc. Edinr

IMPROVED ROADS.

The rebellion of 1745 gave the first great impetus to the formation of good roads in England. The Highlanders who carried no luggage had been able to penetrate to almost the centre of England before any information of their movements was known in the metropolis. They were nimble-footed, and outstripped the cavalry and artillery of the Royal army, which were continually delayed by almost impassable roads. After the suppression of the rebellion, Government directed its attention to the permanent subordination of the Highlands. The construction of good roads was considered indispensable to this project, and after that time the main high roads between north and south were constructed, and wheeled vehicles gradually came into general use.

The following, bearing date Nov. 24th, 1790, gives an idea of what were then termed

EXPEDITIOUS WAGGONS.

In ten days from Carlisle to London, and the same in return by way of York every week. Messrs. Handleys respectfully inform their friends and the public in general that they have erected stage waggons which leave Carlisle early on Tuesday morning and arrive at York on Thursday night, and Leeds on Saturday morning (where goods for all parts in the south are regularly forwarded by the respective carriers), arrive at the White Bear, Bassinghall Street, on Friday night, and set out every Monday night, and arrive at and leave York on Tuesday morning, Bedal, Richmond, Barnard Castle, Burgh, Appleby, Penrith, and arrive at Carlisle on Friday evening, where goods are immediately forwarded to Wigton, Cockermouth, Workington, Whitehaven, and any other place in Cumberland; also to Annan, Dumfries, Glasgow, Edinburgh, Aberdeen, and all other principal towns in Scotland. They hope by their attention to business to merit the favours of all those who please to employ them. N.B. — Their waggon leaves Sheffield on Saturday, and Leeds on Monday. For further particulars apply to Robert Wilson, bookkeeper, or J. Birkett, innkeeper, Carlisle.

A GOOD JOKE.

The following story is on record of the Oxford coach, Defiance:
— Term was over, the coach was full of young Oxonians returning
to their respective colleges, the morning was cold, wet, and
miserable, and the well-appointed drag drove up to the White
Horse Cellar, Piccadilly. 'Have you any room inside?' asked
as pretty a girl as you could wish to see on a summer's day.
'What a beauty,' exclaimed one. 'Quite lovely,' said another.
'Perfect,' lisped a third. 'Quite full, Miss, inside and out,' replied the coachman. 'Surely you could make room for one,'
persisted the fair applicant. 'Quite impossible without the
young gentlemen's consent.' 'Lots of room,' cried the insides,
'we are not very large, we can manage to take one more.' 'If
the gentlemen consent,' replied the driver, 'I can have no
objection.' 'We agree,' said the inside quartette. 'All right,'
responded the coachman. The fare was paid, and the guard
proceeded to open the door and let down the steps. 'Now
Miss, if you please, we are behind our time.' 'Come grandfather,' replied the damsel, addressing a most respectable looking
portly elderly man, 'the money is paid, get in, and be sure you
thank the young gentlemen;' at the same time, suiting the action
to the word, and with a smile assisting her respected grandfather
into the coach. 'Here's some mistake, you'll squeeze us to
death,' cried the astonished party. 'Sorry to incommode you,'
replied the intruder, 'but I hope you won't object to have both
windows up, I'm sadly troubled with a cough.' At this moment
'All right, sit fast,' was heard, and the Defiance rattled away,
drowning the voices of the astonished Oxonians.

EARLY MAIL COACHES.

The mail coaches were chocolate bodied, picked out with
red ; the wheels, perch, waist, bars and pole all scarlet, with a
royal coat of arms on the panel of the door. They were constructed to carry four inside and four out. The mail bags were
placed on the roof. There was a round seat behind, where the
guard sat, covered with skin ; and pockets for pistols were
placed on each side. A blunderbuss was also carried as pro-
tection against robbers.

COACH HORSES.

It was one of the early objections to the introduction of railways that horses in consequence would be but little required; that it would no longer pay to bring up good animals, and that the splendid breed of horses must necessarily die out. I find that the price of coach horses, say 50 years ago, was : — For wheelers, required to measure at least 'fifteen, one,' from £22 to £25 per head, on the average, but never more than £30. Lighter horses were used as leaders, and could be bought for a few pounds less per head. Most of the horses came from Ireland, and were picked up at the large fairs held at Rossley Hill and Brough Hill. If we compare the general price of horses in the old coaching days with that of the present time, we find they are now much dearer, and the same class of animals as were used half a century ago for coaching purposes are now worth from £10 to £15 a head more than then. Thus we see that instead of spoiling that branch of trade, horses have gradually become dearer since the time of railways, and really good animals will at all times command a market.

A GOOD-TEMPERED COACHMAN.

'Nimrod' tells a good story of the London and Chester, 'Highflyer,' which started at eight o'clock in the morning, and arrived at Chester about the same time in the evening : distance 40 miles. This was always a good road for wheels, and rather favourable for draught. How, then, could all these hours be accounted for? Why, if a commercial gentleman wanted to pay a morning visit, there could be no objection to that. In the pork-pie season half an hour was generally occupied in consuming one of them, for Mr. Williams, the coachman, was a wonderful favourite with the farmers' wives and daughters all along the road. The coach dined at Wrexham, and Wrexham Church was to be seen, a fine specimen of the florid Gothic, and one of the wonders of Wales. Then Wrexham was also famous for ale, there being no public breweries in those days in Wales, and above all the inn belonged to Sir Watkin. About two hours were allowed for dinner, but Billy Williams, one of the best-tempered fellows on earth, and as honest as Aristides, was never

GRASMERE from RED BANK

to half an hour or so. 'The coach is ready, gentlemen, but don't let me disturb you if you wish for another bottle.' The leisurely way in which things were done in those days affords a powerful contrast to the high pressure movements of our own times, and a day of 12 hours was formerly spent in travelling between the two towns before mentioned, the distance being 40 miles. It need not now take more than half the time to travel between one town and the other, and return after having had a fair time to transact ordinary business.

* THE MAIL.

The up mails, which left Carlisle at six o'clock in the evening, reached London at five o'clock on the second morning. The fare was £6 6s. inside, and £3 5s. out. Fees to the coachman and guard brought up the expenses considerably. The coachman's fees were supposed to be two shillings for 50 miles, and some of them made as much as £300 a year, but it was light come light go with them, and few contrived to save any money. They were strictly the contractors' servants, and looked after the passengers' luggage. The guards, who were servants of Government, had full charge of the mail and bags. They were supplied with chronometers, and kept the time not only for the coaches, but all down the road the clocks and watches were timed by the guard's watch. The appointment was obtained through members of Parliament with the Postmaster General of the day. An inspector travelled four days a week on the mails, and reported weak harness; and the guards, who had half a guinea a week, made all their reports through him. This seems but small pay, but perquisites made up their earnings considerably.

THE FIRST COACH FROM KESWICK.

It may be interesting to the people of Keswick to know that the late Mr. Banks, of Shu-le-Crow, tanner, was the first man to start a coach from Keswick, it ran to Cockermouth and back daily, over the Whinlatter Pass. This was in the year 1822, before the new road to Cockermouth by Bassenthwaite Lake was made. Bob McCade, better known as Bob Kegg, was the driver.

* See 'Saddle and Sirloin.'

He was a noted character in his day, and is still remembered by many in Keswick. A few years after, Jack Hayes drove an opposition coach from Keswick to Whitehaven. A coach also ran between Carlisle and Keswick, via Wigton, driven by a noted whip named Jack Cawx. Jack claimed the honour of driving the first chaise into Borrowdale. The road at that time was very bad, and he had a narrow escape from upsetting his carriage near Grange Bridge. This was in the year 1824. The mail coaches were horsed by contract, and tenders were invited every year, although the contractors did not often change their ground.

THE LATE MR. TEATHER, formerly of the Royal Oak, Keswick, and his father before him, were both well-known on the road. Mr. Teather, senr., some fifty years ago, was the principal mail contractor in the north of England, his head-quarters being Carlisle, and from this centre he horsed the mail coaches in various directions. He had, among other contracts, the working of the mail coach between Carlisle and Glasgow, a distance of 96 miles; the journey occupied about nine hours. He also worked the coaches as far south as Lancaster. At this time 80 horses were kept at the different coaching houses in the Border City, and they worked eight mail and seven stage coaches. The introduction of railways had the effect of considerably reducing Mr. Teather's business, and towards the latter part of his time he handed over what remained of it to his son. The iron horse in time drove him off the road also, and he left Carlisle and commenced business as hotel keeper at the Royal Oak, Keswick. The last contract was in connection with Mr. Gelderd, of Patterdale, for the mail coaches between Windermere and Cockermouth.

FROM KENDAL TO WHITEHAVEN.

In the old coaching days the head-quarters of the coaches which ran through Keswick were Kendal and Whitehaven, the distance between those two towns being performed in a day, Ambleside, Keswick, and Cockermouth being merely places of

call This is shown by the following coaching bill of the
period :—

Light   Post   Coach.

The Good Intent,

From Kendal to Whitehaven,

Runs from

The King's Arms Inn, Kendal,

Every Tuesday, Thursday, and Saturday morning, at half-past
five o'clock, by way of Ambleside, Keswick, and Cockermouth ;
Workington to Whitehaven, where it arrives the same evening :
returns from Whitehaven every Wednesday, Friday, and Sunday morning at eight o'clock, and arrives at the King's Arms,
Kendal, about half-past eight o'clock. Passengers will have the
opportunity of the following coaches the next day at Kendal, viz :
The Leeds coach, at five o'clock in the morning.

The Liverpool and Manchester heavy coach, at three o'clock in
the morning.

The Liverpool and Manchester mail coaches at ten o'clock
in the morning and two o'clock in the afternoon. Performed by

John Jackson, King's Arms, Kendal.

William Wilcock, Salutation Inn, Ambleside.

John I'Anson, Royal Oak, Keswick.

William Wood, Globe, Cockermouth.

N.B. — The proprietors request permission to observe that
they will not be answerable for more than five pounds for any
box, parcel, truss. or luggage, if lost or damaged, unless entered
as valuable, and insured accordingly. — Sept. 1st, 1811.

COACHING   ACCIDENTS.

Though accidents in our modern mode of travelling are of too
frequent occurrence, it is questionable whether the percentage is
greater than in the more primitive mode of coaching. The
Cumberland Pacquet contained the account of an accident to
the Over Sands coach in 1811 : 'On Wednesday, the 7th, a very
distressing accident happened on the Cartmel sands. As the
Lancaster stage coach was crossing the Kent channel the horses
turned restive, in consequence of which the coach remained

DERWENT WATER

from Castle Head

stationary, and the current at the same time running briskly, washed away the sand which supported the wheels on one side, and the coach formed so deep a hole that it was literally turned the wrong side up. There were fifteen passengers within and without. The outside passengers were precipitated into the channel, and the inside passengers after escaping through the windows were left at the mercy of the stream. One young lady was carried down a considerable distance, and was with much difficulty saved: she is at present lying at Kent's Bank, with little hopes of recovery. An old gentleman was dragged out of the water quite senseless; a woman and her two children were washed from the top of the coach, and were in great danger of drowning. All the loose luggage was washed away: two pointer dogs which were in the boot remained engulped in the sand with the coach. There seems little chance of recovering the coach.' A Lancaster paper, in referring to the accident, a week later, says that nothing was recovered of the vehicle, and after expressing the good fortune of the passengers on being extricated from their awful and perilous situation, concludes by noting that 'nearly twenty years have elapsed since a similar accident happened on these sands.'

THE OLD 'COACHEY.'

Coach drivers were much opposed to railways; they were not slow to see that the road must eventually give way to the rail, and then their calling would be gone. An old coachman used to caution his passengers in the following way:—'Don't yer travel by those new-fangled steam engines. Suppose you travel by my coach, and you meets with an accident? There you are! But suppose you travel by rail, and you meets with an accident? Where are ye?' The coach driver was generally popular on the road. He was a great man with the farmers' wives and daughters along his route; he executed many small commissions for them in the market town, and was considered quite a responsible man. The sound of his horn was inspiriting: on hearing its mellow notes everyone was on the alert to see the coach pass. When he drove up to the inn where the coach changed horses, there might be seen the usual assemblage of people attracted by business or curiosity.   Besides, the sight of a well-loaded coach with four good horses will always command the approbation of the crowd.   The 'coacheys' in those days lived on the fat of the land.   Always one hot joint, if not two, awaited the arrival of the coach, and the twenty minutes allotted for the refreshment of the inner man were, as a rule, thoroughly utilised; though I have heard it asserted there were times when the soup was made so hot that the unfortunate passenger, in consequence of waiting till it cooled, was but half way through his dinner when it was announced that the coach was ready for starting.   What was called the 'road game' was a source of great amusement.   It was generally played by the coachman and the person sitting beside him.   They first tossed for the choice of which side of the road they would have ; then each counted what was met on his side.   A donkey counted seven, a pig one, a black sheep one, a cat five, a cat in a window ten, a dog one, a magpie one, a grey horse five, and there was one thing by which the game was won at once, but this was of rare occurrence, I cannot venture to describe it, but can imagine the roars of laughing and the shouts of 'game's up,' when such a thing actually took place.

TOM PRESTON. — Most people who have lived up to middle age will remember Tom Preston and David Johnson.   They were the last men who drove coaches through Keswick under the old *regime*.   The guards of these coaches, Arnold and Burnett, were also very well known.   Before the railway interfered with coaching arrangements one of the drivers started from Lancaster and the other from Whitehaven every morning, taking with them the mails.   The journey between the two towns was accomplished in something like 12½ hours, distance 81½ miles.   Towards the latter part of their time the journey by coach was considerably shortened, the railway having reached Windermere at one end of the road and Cockermouth at the other.   Tom Preston is still remembered for his kind and obliging disposition.   He was a general favourite on the road.   If the farmers' wives alongside his route required any shopping done for them in Keswick or Ambleside they knew they could rely on Tom to do it, seeing that he was always ready and willing to serve them. As a reward for services thus rendered, a sausage or some other tit-bit from the larder was generally handed up to him on the box.

DAVID JOHNSON, although a decent, steady-going man, could not be said to enjoy the same popularity as his *confrere*. He had not been brought up to coach-driving in his youth, having been during his early days in a gentleman's service. It was said he was not able to acquit himself with the 'ribbons' in the same style as Tom Preston. It was David Johnson's coach that came in collision with the poet Wordsworth's pony chaise a short distance to the south of Roughhow bridge in Naddle, Arnold being guard at the time. A contributor to Frazer's Magazine for August, 1850, which was some few years after the accident happened, gives the following account of it in Arnold's own words. Arnold at that time had given up his place as coach-guard, and was landlord of the Ferry Hotel, Windermere, the writer staying with him at the time, as guest. To the enquiry by one of the company if he knew the poet Wordsworth, 'Knowed him,' he said, with a merry twinkle in his eye, 'I should think I did a few,' and rising from his seat he reached and took down a tin horn from beside the beam that ran along the ceiling. 'That' said he, eyeing the instrument with a look of affection, 'was when I blowed the horn.' So saying he gave it a blast that smacked of the coaching days of old. What blowing the horn had to do with his knowledge of the poet was a puzzle to those of the company who had never heard his story before, which included myself and a yachtsman. 'Blowed the horn,' said the latter, 'what do you mean by that?' 'Why, you see, this is the way I comed to knaw Wadsworth, and I shan't forget in a hurry. When I was guard to the Whitehaven Mail, five years agone and more, as we were slapping along and just coming to a sharpish turn, ye knaw the corner by the bridge three miles this side o' Keswick, what should we see but sumthin tall and grand tooling along a little pony shay as cool a murder. "Oh! Lor, here's a smash," says I, and afore the words were out o' mi mouth crash went the shay all to smithereens, right through a dry wall, and slap went the driver

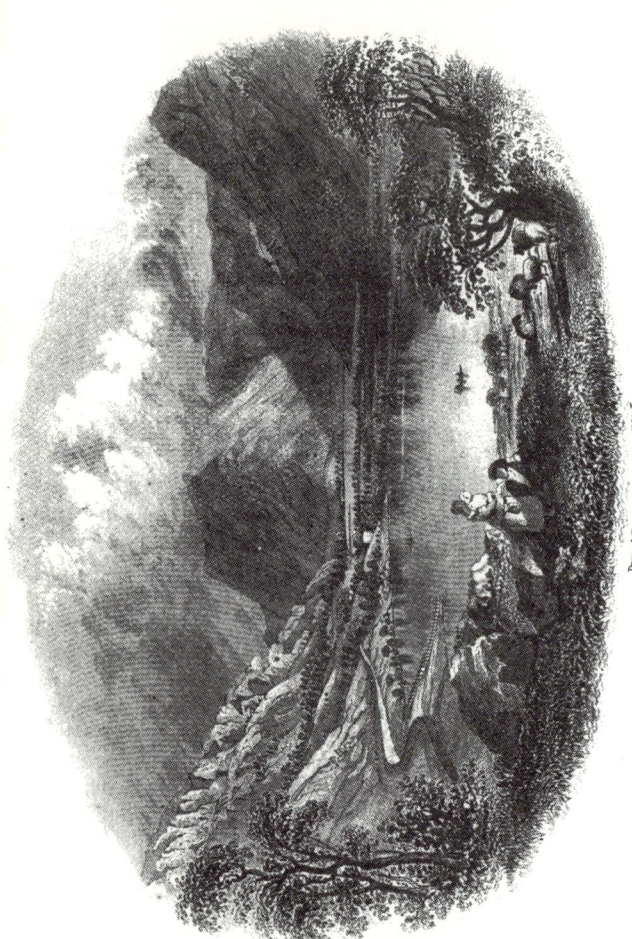

Drawn & Engᵈ by T.Banks & Son Edinᵇ

CRUMMOCK & BUTTERMERE LAKES

over into a plantation, arms out and great coat a-flying. We thought for sure it was all over with im, but presently he picked hissel up uncommon tall again, and says he, "I'll have this matter thoroughly investigated." With that he walked off towards the public, and "Jem," said coachee to I, very down like, for 'twas a bad bit o' business, "who do you think that is!" "Who! who!! Davey," says I. "Why who but the powit Wadsworth?" And now gentlemen,' says he, turning round, 'when you next go to Keswick, just by the bridge about three miles out, you'll see two yards of the wall down to this day, and that's where we spilt the poet.' A prolonged blast on the horn marked the landlord's sense of the excellence of the joke. 'Aye, an' often an' often,' continued he, returning the horn to its place, 'since that I've seen the grand folks draw up to the mount, I've said sly like to myself, "Ah, gentlemen, you be a going to see the powit, but you never had'n call upon you unexpected like, on a flying visit over a wall.'

PARSON BIRD, who lived at Braithwaite Lodge, near Keswick, was fond of coaching and was a very clever whip. He was on friendly terms with the driver of a coach which at that time ran through Keswick called 'The Cuckoo.' He sometimes rode a mile or two alongside the coach to see how the horses worked. Mrs. Bleamire, of Derwent Bank, who had noticed the Parson's little hobby, one day met him when riding behind the coach, when she exclaimed to him that it was very strange that the Cuckoo was *always* followed by a little Bird. For several weeks during one winter Parson Bird, who was a man of humane feelings, drove the coach running between Whitehaven and Lancaster, and handed over the fees to the regular driver, who at the time was laid up with a broken leg. A lady rode with him one evening, the coach stopped at the Turk's Head, Kendal, and she then left the coach, presenting the driver with half-a-crown. A ball was held in Kendal the same evening, and great was the surprise of the lady passenger when one of the first to whom she was introduced was the man who had driven the coach. At this she was indignant, remarking that she was come of a good family and had

L. Aspland Del.

W. Banks Sc. Edin?

UPPER REACH OF ULLSWATER

more respect for herself than to dance with a coach driver. However, when the matter was explained, she thought much better of it, so much so that in less than twelve months she became Mrs. Bird.

JACK SHELDON. — Many people in Keswick, and other parts of the Lake district, remember Jack Sheldon. He drove, for some years, the coach between Windermere and Keswick; also, at times, drove one running between Keswick and Patterdale.* 'Now, gentlemen,' he would say to his passengers, 'as you have come all the way from London to see this beautiful scenery, you would of course like to know the names of the hills, mountains, knolls, and rivers, we call them 'becks' about here for shortness. Well, gentlemen, that wooded hill on the left is Mell Fell, a rare place for birds' nesting, black-berrying, and nutting. The hill behind us is Saddleback, called by some Blencathra. Looking straight along the line of rail, you see Newlands Dod in the beautiful vale of Newlands, the hill on the left of it is Catbells, uprising from the shores of the charming Derwentwater, and the three round-headed undulating hills on our left hand, form the back of poetical Helvellyn. You don't see as much of Helvellyn from this side as the other. I've driven under the shadow of Helvellyn thousands of times. The mountain begins at Dunmail Raise above Grasmere, and ends in the poetical vale of St. John, a distance of seven miles. Sir Walter Scott's poem, " I climed the dark brow of the mighty Helvellyn," is familiar to everyone, and the vale of St. John is named in the Bridal of Triermain. This is Matterdale Moor we are now crossing, the farmers having a right of grazing so many sheep by paying a shilling a year to the lord of the manor. There's fine grass here and on Helvellyn for the hogs.' " I don't see any hogs," said a retired pork butcher who was 'doing the tourist.' 'Well,' said John, 'not pigs, but you see the small sheep running about; they are a peculiar breed, very hardy and very sweet eating, and are called 'hogs' for the first year, and when stripped of their fleece they are called 'twinters,' and when stripped of their second fleece they are called 'thrunters,' so that's pretty near to

* See 'English Lakes and Mountains.'

WINDERMERE LAKE
from "Road to Ulverstone."

'grunters,' but when killed they are called by the butcher
"Helvellyn mutton."'

Jack wrote the following quaint lines about the Ullswater
coach : —

'Arriving at Troutbeck without botheration,
Ask for Jack Sheldon's coach, (crack whip), at the station.
Two and sixpence you'll own is a moderate fare,
To be driven to Patterdale, Devil-me-Care ;
He'll point out each mountain and beck in the vales
Of Matterdale, Dockwray, Glencoin, Patterdale,
Describe all the wonders ever heard of or seen,
And jingle his jokes too, all right, all serene.'

It is related Jack had, at the time when he drove the 'Opposition,' a race down Castlerigg Brow with the regular
coach. He was close behind his rival when they reached the
junction of the roads where there is now the toll gate, and Jack
took the road leading to Keswick by Brigholm, galloping all the
way, the other coach going by Brow Top ; the race into the
town was so close that a collision nearly occurred at the Royal
Oak corner, where the driver of the regular coach triumphantly shot past right in front of Jack. Jack then drove to one of
the hotels where a gentleman — his only passenger — who had
been nearly terrified to death, and was making tracks as fast as
he could. Jack was soon up to him. 'Please sir, remember
the coachman.' 'Yes, I'll remember you,' exclaimed the man,
'and that to the last day of my life, but never more will I ride
with you.' Jack was the first man to introduce coaching to
Buttermere about 20 years ago. Although the road is now very
rough, it was much more so at that time, and it was looked on
as being something like a feat to drive a carriage and pair over
Honister Pass to Buttermere. He was not, however, allowed to
have this business to himself very long. Some of the principal
hotel keepers joined, and a coach was announced to run to Buttermere via Honister Pass, every day in the week, Sundays excepted. I need hardly say that coaching to Buttermere has
greatly developed of late years. That beautiful valley now
acts as a show place for Keswick, and on fine days in summer,
scores of tourists leave the different hotels in Keswick, *en route*

Drawn & Engraved by W. Banks & Son, Edinr

BOWNESS, FROM BELLE ISLE, WINDERMERE.

for Buttermere, via Borrowdale and Honister Pass, returning by the vale of Newlands. There has been much improvement of late years in the vehicles used for the Buttermere excursions. A waggonette to hold 10 or 12 was, till a few years ago, styled a Buttermere coach. Chars-a-bancs, built for the purpose, are now in general use, and give much more satisfaction to the tourists.

JIMMY TELFER, who drove on several stages in the North of England was a well-known careful driver and was always punctuality itself. Any passengers intending to travel by his coach might be thankful if he were not left behind, supposing he was but a very short time after the time of starting. He was known to be crusty at times, but always very straightforward. The following lines were composed on the Leeds Coach coming from Kirkby Lonsdale to Kendal upon a remark of Telfer's. The remark referred to was made by a man, who being asked to put on the drag, found it rather warm.

> 'A coachman one day coming down a long hill
> Where he'd put on a drag for fear he should spill,
> Asked a man who was passing if he'd be so kind
> As to put up the drag, that was lying behind ;
> The fellow soon seized it, but not by the chain,
> And presently after he dropped it again.
> "Is it rather too heavy," says Jimmy, " or what ?"
> "Nay, heavy be hanged, why the thing is red hot."'

TOM HARRISON, who died last spring, was a well known coachman. He drove Mr. Rigg's Windermere and Keswick coach for upwards of twenty years. He was very genial in his manner, and in addition to his usefulness in pointing out places of interest along the road he could amuse the coach passengers by telling them funny stories. Mr. Roger Gresley, a commercial traveller and who, some years ago was well known on the road as Sir Roger, was a great friend of Tom Harrison's, and many a time during a journey over the Raise have they had contests at spinning yarns, to the amusement of their fellow-passengers. Harrison used to tell a story of Sir Roger in something like the following style : ' I was coming ower t'Raise wi' t'evening coach, Sir Roger and a friend of his sitting beside me on't box and other four gentlemen on't seat behind, all as good sorts as you need wish to meet : we'd just commenced telling tailes when we got to Threspot — they keep good beer at Threspot, King's Head Inn, you know — so we all got off t'coach to have refreshment. Before we got on't coach again Sir Roger called me aside, and said to me "Tom, if thou'll give me eighteen pence I'll put thee on a good thing." I wondered what he was going to be up to, but I knew he was a good sort, so I gave him eighteen pence. Well, when we were fairly on't road Sir Roger commenced his queer tailes again, and we nearly all had a turn before getting to Keswick. I told them two or three of t' real old fashioned sort, and made them roar wi laughing. When t' coach drew up at t' Royal Oak, Sir Roger said, ' Now, gentlemen, we must remember the coachman." He showed the company half-a-crown, and then put it in my hand — a shilling is the coachman's due you know, we have no wages — but that night I got half-crowns instead of shillings, as t' company all followed suit to Sir Roger. He's dead and gone, but he was a good sort.' Harrison was a man who did not possess the advantage of any school education ; probably owing to his almost daily companionship with men of education, he was able, to a certain extent, to imitate their style of conversation, but no one, unacquainted with his history would have ever suspected that he was unable to either read or write. He was of a careful disposition, and very shrewd in business matters. During the time he drove the Windermere and Keswick coach he contrived to save a considerable amount of money, at the time of his death being worth about £4,000.

ERNEST HARGREAVES, ESQ. — During the summer of 1881 Mr. Ernest Hargreaves, a gentleman from Tunbridge Wells, introduced the London style of coaching into the lake district. He made Bowness his head quarters, and drove from there *via* Windermere to Keswick and back every day. His coach, which was called 'The Sportsman,' was purchased from the celebrated builder, Holland, of London, and was similar in construction to those made use of by the members of the Coaching and Four-in-hand Clubs. The coach was worked by a stud of twenty-one spanking horses, many of them thoroughbreds; relays of these were kept at different places along the road, and the coach changed its teams three times on the journey out and in. Mr. Hargreaves was always particular in having his horses turned out scrupulously clean, the same with the harness, which was brass-mounted and made expressly to order, and ill-fared the stable man if the buckles and turrets and other parts of the harness were not turned out as bright as a new pin. Mr. Hargreaves' object in bringing his dashing team to the lake district was for the purpose of qualifying himself to be a member of the Coaching Club. To be eligible for election, a candidate is required to drive so many thousand miles without an accident. It was, of course, impossible for the amateur coachman to constantly 'tool his own team,' but he had a good right-hand man in Billy Crosthwaite, who was an old professional, well known on the road, and who took turns with his master in holding the ribbons. George Marriner, who wore a red coat, acted as guard, and looked over the general management all round. The coach was fairly patronised by the tourists, and Mr. Hargreaves, although very successful, would have been much more so had his health not broken down before the end of the season ; this made him decide on giving up coaching till such time as his health was again fully established. It was intended that the Sportsman should have run again last summer, but the enterprise was abandoned.

HOW TO DRIVE.

The following appeared in *Land and Water:*

Sir,—My son is perfectly crazy about driving four-in-hand. Hang the expense, he says, &c., &c. His governor seems full of money, for he goes on to say that 'I don't mind.' Something like a governor, but whatever you or your governor may do, do not pretend to drive till you can catch your whip properly. Nothing seems so cocktail or muffish on a coach as to see a man learning to catch his whip, and after many futile attempts taking it upside down for this purpose, and twisting the thong round and round as if he were stirring porridge for a pack of hounds. But how is a fellow to learn to catch his whip? you may say. To this I reply, if you are such an awkward fellow as not to be able to learn to catch it, and almost by instinct, shut yourself up in your own room, put a chair upon your table, harness four chairs together, get a stiff top joint of your fishing-rod, if you have one, or any light stick that will do duty for one, plait some whipcord, and make a thong twice as long as your stick ; and, having seated yourself on a chair for a box, learn to catch your whip there, and in private, and learn to hit your horses all round. They cannot run away or upset your coach if you are careful ; catch up your thong and hit your wheelers, then untwist it and hit your leaders, first on the off-side, it is easiest to begin with ; then on the near side, first the one and the other — one, two, three, and a draw, and so on the other side. You may in these days never be called upon to hit a horse at all, but you ought to be able to do it, and if you can't do it you are not a coachman, though you may fancy you are, and getting on pretty well with a flash team in Hyde Park, where you have nothing to do but hold your reins and steer clear of your friends and neighbours.

COACHES STILL POPULAR IN THE DISTRICT.

Travelling by coach is very popular in the lake district, judging from the fact that it was announced in the local papers a year or two ago that no less than sixteen well appointed coaches left Windermere and Bowness daily (Sundays excepted), for various points in the district, and these were so well patronised that frequently two or three extra ones were required. The roads in many parts of the district are still in a very primitive state, quite dangerous, if not impossible to drive carriages over, and altogether behind the time. The English Lake District Association is now every year using its best endeavours to remedy this state of things ; some good work has already been done ; greater things are projected. This undertaking in now accomplished. A good road will shortly be made over Hard-knott and Wrynose Passes, and in the course of a few years we shall, in all probability, have a road from the Windermere district by Langdale, over the Stake Pass, and down the Borrowdale Valley to Keswick. This will no doubt have the effect of bringing more visitors during the season, and we may expect to see more coaching than ever in the district.

THE PALMY DAYS OF COACHING.

In looking back to what is termed the palmy days of coaching we are sometimes apt to compare the past with the present mode of travelling. To be seated outside a coach in fine summer weather is always enjoyable; but in the old days the fast coaches travelled night and day in all weathers except when stopped by a fall of snow. When a long journey was contemplated a seat on the coach had to be booked a week beforehand, and half the fare deposited. To travel during winter on bitterly cold nights with limbs benumbed, or to sit for hours together in a drenching rain, were vicissitudes which befel all regular coach travellers. By coach from Carlisle to London occupied two nights and one day fifty years ago, when the coaching-system was worked in its greatest perfection. We can now take a seat in a luxurious railway carriage, where we can read, smoke, or sleep, or amuse ourselves in numberless ways, and perform the journey from Carlisle to the Metropolis in less than eight hours, in fact, by the time a coach could have reached Preston. But, in spite of these advantages, the innate love of the English people for horse-flesh is such that they will always appreciate a good four-in-hand, and so long as the lake district retains its present charming views and drives, there is no doubt that wherever a coach-route is formed, with well-found coaches, good cattle, and punctual service, the public will duly appreciate those advantages, and the promoters will never have cause to regret having provided one of the most enjoyable pleasures of the day, more especially for the dwellers in large cities, to whom the bracing effects of a drive on a good four-in-hand cannot fail to be beneficial both to body and mind, as the ever-varying scenes, impossible to be obtained on a railway, must give relief to the over-worked brain; and at the same time the fresh air renovates the body and fits the tourist for renewed exertions, and he can again commence work with light spirits after his holidays are ended.

ADDENDA.

'A Kendalian' writing to the Editor of the *West Cumberland Times* says :—

'Sir,—In common with most of your readers, I read Mr. Wilson's article with much pleasure. Perhaps you will allow me space to say what I have seen of coaches and coach drivers.

I knew Jack Sheldon and his brother William well. Jack was my favourite as a driver, and in watching him mount the "Engineer," which started from the Crown Inn, Kendal (William Dixon, landlord), I was sure there was something in the wind. As soon as the word was given "all right," Jack lightly touched his three horses, and with a final point rounded the corner of the street—(then the old Pump Inn) —a most awkward place, and off he went at a rapid rate. Indeed, I had never seen previously a coach go so fast. The consequence was when Jack got the "Engineer" in the middle of Stramongate, opposite Dr. Tatham's, he was going on two wheels. He found it so, and settled a little while he came to Stramongate Bridge. Up and over, and away he went full drive, his object being to pass the mail (North Britain) that had only gone five minutes before. Jack overtook the mail about the first mile-stone, and his heart revived, and he was happy again.

Jack, in his flying coach, flew over on the 24th February, 1844, on Shap Fell, and got into a sad scrape; and like Bob Dover, who drove down Huck's Brow from Shap Fell at a gallop, he got the frowns and dislikes of the coaching public, some of whom would not travel where these two were to handle the reins of the particular coach they intended to patronise in their journey.

I remember watching the last run of the Whitehaven coach, from the Commercial Hotel, at Kendal, on the 28th May, 1847, driven by Tom Preston, with Arnold the guard, who played his bugle in his best fashion, and the waving of banners and the shaking of the heads of the old English gentleman, looking at the end of prosperous days, and the advent of a killing age.

Mr. Wilson omitted to name an old Jehu in the person of 'Jimmy Blenkhorn,' who was the only well-to-do coach-driver Kendal ever could boast of among the many. After the Lancaster and Carlisle line was opened "James" drove one or other of the many Lake District coaches, and must have driven to Keswick some time or other, though his name appears to be forgotten.

I am, sir, yours truly,

A KENDALIAN.

THE KESWICK HOTEL

The Keswick Hotel, Bridge and River Greta.

WILLIAM WILSON, Lessee

THIS Hotel, the largest and most commodious in the Lake District, stands in its own grounds of several acres, on the banks of the river Greta, and near to Lake Derwentwater; *it commands the finest and most extensive views of the surrounding scenery,* and the mountains of Scafell Pike, Helvellyn, and Skiddaw (the three highest in the district), are distinctly visible from the Coffee-room windows. The Hotel is also within easy distance of all the Cumberland Lakes, and most of those in Westmorland. Visitors have permission to fish in the Greta. Telegraph and Telephone on the premises. A spacious Drawing-room for ladies is attached to the Coffee-room.

ADJOINING THE RAILWAY STATION AND CONNECTED BY A
CORRIDOR.

OVERLOOKING THE NEW FITZ PARK.

TENNIS COURTS. POST HORSES AND MOUNTAIN PONIES.